ROMAN BRITAIN

Jenny Hall and Christine Jones

Designed by
Sarah Peden

Edited by
Alison Cooper

Picture Research by
Helen Taylor

Illustrated by
Lorraine Harrison, Sally Hynard, Ray Grinaway and Peter Kesteven from The Garden Studio Illustration Agency

The assistance of the Museum of London and Colchester Museums in the preparation of this book is gratefully acknowledged

CONTENTS

The Roman Empire

1 The legend
Romans believe the story that the founder of Rome was a man called Romulus.

2 The beginning of Rome
Villages are built on seven hills near the River Tiber. The villages grow larger and join to form the city of Rome.

3 Rome becomes a republic
At first, Rome is ruled by kings. Then Roman citizens expel their last king, Tarquin the Proud.

4 Conquests
The Roman republic grows as Rome's armies conquer surrounding states. They eventually rule all of Italy.

c. **753** BC   *c.* **510** BC   25
B

The Roman Empire in the second century AD

Look at the names of the Roman provinces. Can you see any that are similar to the names we use for the countries today?

5 Enemies of Rome
Wars with Greece and Carthage in north Africa. Hannibal, the Carthaginian general, fails to capture Rome. The power of Rome spreads beyond Italy.

6 Civil wars
Rome's leaders fight among themselves. These wars stop when Julius Caesar becomes dictator. He is later murdered and the fighting starts again.

7 The first emperor
Rivals again battle for leadership. Augustus defeats Mark Antony and soon becomes ruler. The Roman Empire is created.

8 Birth of Jesus Christ
Jesus lives in Palestine, a province of the Roman Empire. He is crucified by the Romans.

:02 BC

44 BC

27 BC

9 The Empire grows larger
The descendants of Augustus conquer more lands.

BC or AD?
The dates in this book are marked BC or AD. Today, in the west, we use the Christian way of counting years. The years Before Christ was born are marked BC. The years after the birth of Christ have AD in front of them, standing for the Latin words *Anno Domini*, which mean 'in the year of Our Lord'. The Romans had different ways for counting years.

AD 43

10 Britannia – a new province
Emperor Claudius invades Britain. Other countries become provinces of the Empire.

AD 200

11 Time of unrest
Barbarians attack outlying provinces and Roman leaders battle to become Emperor. Many Christians are put to death for their belief in one god, until AD 312 when Emperor Constantine becomes a Christian.

AD 337

12 The Empire is divided into two after the Emperor Constantine dies
The Empire in the East, called Byzantium, is ruled from Constantinople (now Istanbul, Turkey).

AD 410

13 The Empire crumbles
Britain ceases to be part of the Empire. Rome is attacked by barbarians and the Western Empire collapses. The eastern half, Byzantium, continues until AD 1453.

AD 1453

The first invasion

In 55 BC, the Roman general Julius Caesar sailed with his army across the Channel from France to Britain. Anxious Britons watched the approaching fleet from the clifftops to see what would happen. The Roman soldiers were at first afraid to jump from their boats and go ashore. Eventually, a standard-bearer leapt into the water and waded alone towards the enemy. The Romans would have been disgraced if their standard had fallen into enemy hands - they had to follow.

After winning a few battles against the British tribes in south-east England, Caesar and his army went back to France. The next summer, he returned and there was more fighting. Eventually, some defeated tribes agreed to send tributes (payments) regularly to Rome. Pleased with this, Caesar left. He was the first Roman general to come to Britain but he did not conquer the Britons, nor did the Romans settle in Britain. In fact, they did not return for nearly 100 years, although contacts between Rome and Britain continued.

The Britons

Caesar kept a diary during his campaigns in Britain. From it, historians have been able to find out a lot about what the Britons were like and how they lived and fought.

The Britons lived in groups called tribes. Each tribe lived in a different area of Britain.

Some warriors rode chariots into battle. When near his enemy the warrior leapt from his chariot to fight on foot. If he became tired or was in trouble, his charioteer raced back, so that the warrior could leap on board and be driven to safety.

People lived on farmsteads, growing crops such as wheat, and raising animals for food and clothing. They also hunted and fished. Home-made pottery was hardened in bonfires. British metalworkers were very skilled. They made beautiful objects such as mirrors and jewellery, as well as weapons, and decorated them with swirling, curving patterns.

How do we know?

Finding out about the past is like trying to fit together the pieces of a jigsaw. Archaeologists and historians study objects and writing from Roman times. They try to fit together these pieces of evidence, to understand the whole picture. The jigsaw pieces in this book show some of the evidence that has been found about life in Roman Britain.

This British bronze shield was found in the River Thames at Battersea.

The Roman army

With the help of their well-organised and highly trained army, the Roman leaders were able to conquer many countries, and the Empire spread quickly. The army was divided into legions of foot soldiers. They were skilled in fighting pitched battles and in laying siege to enemy camps. They took great pride in their skills and in their victories. To lose a battle was considered a disgrace.

To help a legion to fight well, it was divided into ten units called cohorts. The first cohort was special, as it was made up of twice as many men as the others. The cohorts were organised into smaller fighting units, the centuries.

				1				Commanding Officer (Legate)		
Deputy Legate			**1**	**1**		Camp Prefect				
		1	**2**	**3**	**4**	**5**	Senior Officers (Tribunes)			
1	**2**	**3**	**4**	**5**	**6**	**7**	**8**	**9**	**10**	Cohorts
5	6	6	6	6	6	6	6	6	6	Centuries
160	80	80	80	80	80	80	80	80	80	Legionary soldiers
x5	x6	x6	x6	x6	x6	x6	x6	x6	x6	
800	480	480	480	480	480	480	480	480	480	TOTAL

Total = 5120 men + officers + 120 mounted scouts and messengers

To defend themselves, legionary soldiers grouped together and made a shell-like defence with their shields. It was called a 'tortoise'.

I am the legate. I am in charge of a legion – about 5500 men.

I am the legion's standard bearer. I carry the eagle which men follow into battle.

I am a centurion, in charge of about 80 men. This unit is called a century.

We are legionary soldie[r]
We carry all the equipm[ent]
we need when on camp
It weighs about 30 kg.

Auxiliary soldiers

The legions were supported by units of auxiliary soldiers, with about 500 men in each unit. These soldiers were often specialist fighters, such as archers, slingers and cavalrymen. Unlike legionary soldiers, auxiliary troops were not citizens of Rome. They were recruited from countries the Romans had conquered.

Pitching camp

When they were away from their base, the soldiers had to pitch camp every night. They dug a deep ditch all around the campsite and placed wooden stakes along the inside edge of the ditch to make a wall. This gave some protection, in case they were attacked. Some soldiers dug latrines and rubbish pits, others collected water and firewood for cooking the evening meal. Their leather tents were big enough for eight men to sleep in.

I am an optio. I carry the standard for a century. We fight together as a group.

I belong to an auxiliary unit of archers.

A sword with its sheath. Can you see the decoration showing the she-wolf that saved Romulus and Remus? Which city was founded by Romulus?

This is the tombstone of Marcus Favonius Facilis. He was a centurion in the Twentieth Legion.

The conquest of Britain

The Emperor Claudius was commander-in-chief of the army – but he was not a soldier. To win the respect of his legions he needed to lead them to victory. The successful invasion of Britain was his way of keeping the soldiers loyal.

In AD 43, about 40 000 soldiers (four legions plus about 20 000 auxiliary soldiers) sailed to Britain and landed near Richborough in Kent. The British tribes fought bravely but were no match for the Romans. The legions fought their way inland from the coast, battled across the River Thames and advanced towards Colchester, the centre of the Catuvellauni tribe.

Emperor and elephants

Aulus Plautius, the Roman general, sent for Claudius. The Emperor came to Britain, bringing with him elephants to amaze and frighten the Britons - they had never seen elephants before. He arrived in time to lead his army into Colchester, where eleven British kings surrendered to him. He then returned to Italy, leaving his legions to conquer the rest of Britain.

The Roman ballista worked like a catapult. It fired iron bolts at the enemy.

Not all the British tribes had surrendered and many continued to fight. The Romans attacked tribal settlements and laid siege to hill-forts. They were too strong for the Britons. Only the tribes in Scotland were able to defy the Romans, and Scotland never became part of the Roman Empire.

The Emperor Claudius had coins made to celebrate his victory over the Britons. This is one of them.

This Briton was killed by an iron arrowhead. Can you see it in his spine?

Maiden Castle was a British hill-fort stormed by Roman soldiers. You can still see the defensive ditches around the hill.

Clues to the past

Beneath modern Colchester, St Albans and London, archaeologists have found evidence of Roman settlements. In all three towns, there is evidence of great fires that destroyed many buildings – houses, shops, and the Temple of Claudius at Colchester.

Archaeologists are like detectives, looking for clues that will help to solve mysteries about the past. The photographs on this page show some of the 'clues' about the fires that archaeologists have been studying. What have they found out?

Burnt pottery and glass from a shop.

The remains of a building in Colchester. The clay wall has been baked hard but the wooden supports have been burnt away, leaving holes in the clay.

Pieces of burnt pottery have been found in many of the buildings. Some of the pottery is stamped with the names of the potters who made it. The archaeologists know that these potters were working in around AD 60. Coins have also been found in the same place - none were made later than AD 60.

The houses and shops of the Roman settlements were built of wood and packed closely together. It is not surprising that fires could spread easily – but it is surprising that all three towns were damaged by fire at the same time. Were the three fires connected?

To find the answer, we have to look elsewhere for help. The Roman writer Tacitus wrote about Britain. His books have been translated from Latin, the language of the Romans, into English. The writing on the scroll tells you what he says about these great fires.

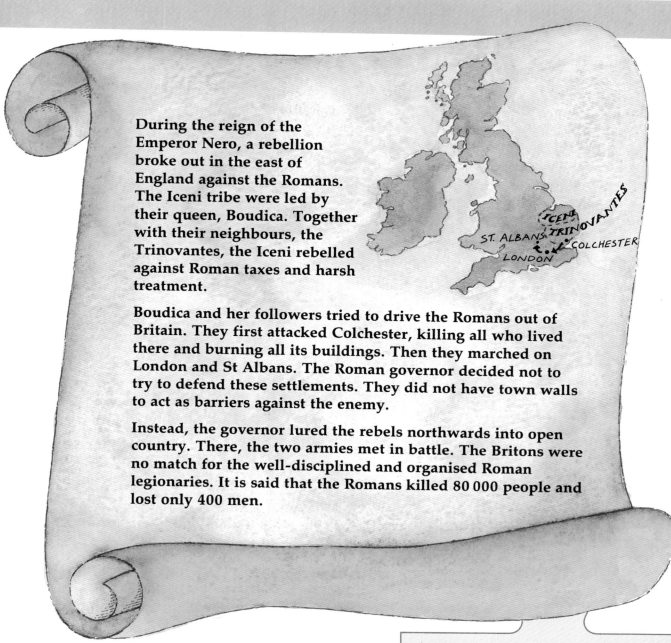

During the reign of the Emperor Nero, a rebellion broke out in the east of England against the Romans. The Iceni tribe were led by their queen, Boudica. Together with their neighbours, the Trinovantes, the Iceni rebelled against Roman taxes and harsh treatment.

Boudica and her followers tried to drive the Romans out of Britain. They first attacked Colchester, killing all who lived there and burning all its buildings. Then they marched on London and St Albans. The Roman governor decided not to try to defend these settlements. They did not have town walls to act as barriers against the enemy.

Instead, the governor lured the rebels northwards into open country. There, the two armies met in battle. The Britons were no match for the well-disciplined and organised Roman legionaries. It is said that the Romans killed 80 000 people and lost only 400 men.

We do not know where this final battle took place, nor do we know for certain what happened to Boudica. She may have poisoned herself after the battle. The Roman governor treated British survivors very badly, but the Emperor Nero sent a wise man called Classicianus to Britain. Classicianus made sure that the Romans ruled the Britons more fairly.

Skulls from London – were these victims of Boudica's attack?

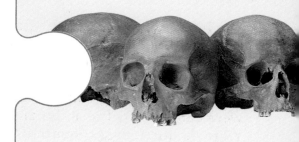

The army at peace

The Roman army was not used only for fighting. Soldiers built forts and fortresses in which to live and a network of good roads, so that the legions could march quickly from place to place. (You can find out more about Roman roads on page 28.) The legions could make for themselves nearly everything they needed to survive in hostile countries. Some soldiers specialised in making and repairing armour, some prepared building materials, others made pottery cooking jars to hold food and drink.

A fortress was big enough to hold an entire legion. Archaeologists have found evidence of legionary bases at Caerleon in Wales, at Inchtuthil in Scotland, and at York, Lincoln, Wroxeter, Colchester, Gloucester and Exeter in England. Settlements often grew up alongside a fortress, where merchants, traders and the families of the soldiers lived.

The Roman governor

The governor was in overall command of a Roman province. He was in charge of the army and it was his job to plan

Workshops in the fortress

campaigns against enemies of the Roman Empire. The governor also had to make sure everyone obeyed Roman laws and paid their taxes. These were sent on to Rome. Legionary soldiers were sometimes chosen to work for the governor.

Hadrian's Wall

The Emperor Hadrian came to Britain in AD 122. He ordered a great wall to be built, to protect the Roman areas of Britain from attack by the tribes in Scotland. It was manned by auxiliary soldiers, who were based in forts and signal turrets built on the Wall.

Many parts of Hadrian's Wall can still be seen today. It is 117 km (80 Roman miles) long and stretches from Bowness to Wallsend.

This legionary soldier's tombstone from London shows him holding writing tablets. He was a clerk who worked for the governor.

In the towns

Before the Roman invasion, Britons lived on farms or inside defended hill-forts. They had no shops and no grand public buildings, nor did they pay taxes to a government far away. The very idea of a town was strange to them. Yet for the Romans, towns were a mark of civilisation. They encouraged all the people they conquered to build and live in towns.

Building the towns

Towns were built to a traditional pattern. Firstly, a clean, regular water supply had to be found. Roads were then laid out, crossing each other at right angles. This produced blocks or 'islands' of land, on which shops and houses were built. On some blocks there were mixes of shops and houses, on others there were only houses - sometimes just one or two splendid ones. Public buildings, such as temples, bath-houses and the town hall (which the Romans called the basilica), were also built within these blocks.

In this photograph taken from an aeroplane, you can see the outline of Roman Silchester still surviving beneath the fields.

A Roman town

basilica

theatre

14

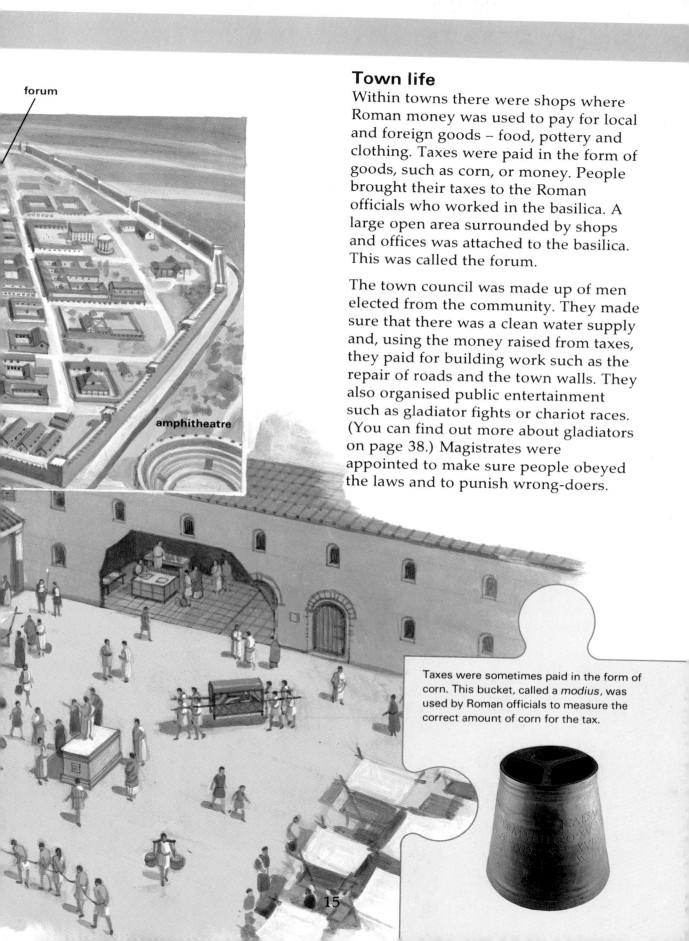

forum

amphitheatre

Town life

Within towns there were shops where Roman money was used to pay for local and foreign goods – food, pottery and clothing. Taxes were paid in the form of goods, such as corn, or money. People brought their taxes to the Roman officials who worked in the basilica. A large open area surrounded by shops and offices was attached to the basilica. This was called the forum.

The town council was made up of men elected from the community. They made sure that there was a clean water supply and, using the money raised from taxes, they paid for building work such as the repair of roads and the town walls. They also organised public entertainment such as gladiator fights or chariot races. (You can find out more about gladiators on page 38.) Magistrates were appointed to make sure people obeyed the laws and to punish wrong-doers.

Taxes were sometimes paid in the form of corn. This bucket, called a *modius*, was used by Roman officials to measure the correct amount of corn for the tax.

Clean and healthy

The Romans knew it was important to have a clean water supply and a clean body. They did not know about germs but they did know that drinking dirty water made people very ill. They drew water from wells and springs and they also used fresh water that was carried by pipes over several kilometres. Drains took away dirty water from bath-houses and public toilets. Most people's houses did not have drains – a toilet was just a bucket or a pot in the kitchen or bedroom.

The baths

The Romans introduced bathing to Britain. Some wealthy people had baths built into their houses but most people went along to the public baths. There, they met friends while sitting in hot rooms, having massages and swimming in the large baths. Strigils were used to scrape off body dirt and sweat, and then sweet-smelling oils were rubbed in.

The most famous Roman baths in Britain are in Bath, Avon. Here there is a temple to Sulis Minerva. She was the goddess associated with the warm-water spring that bubbled into the main bath. This warm water was thought to have healing powers.

A Roman bath-house

Glass oil flask and strigil

The main bath at Bath, today.

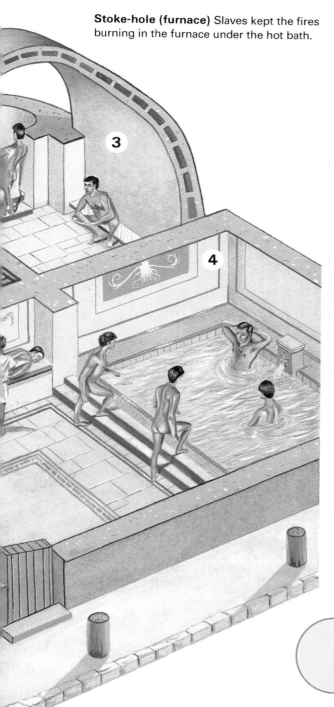

Stoke-hole (furnace) Slaves kept the fires burning in the furnace under the hot bath.

Doctors

Professional doctors were usually Greeks. Bronze scalpels and knives, used for carrying out operations, have been found in Britain. There were also eye doctors who made up their own ointments for patients. Some soldiers had medical skills too, and this is recorded on their tombstones – *medicus ordinarius*.

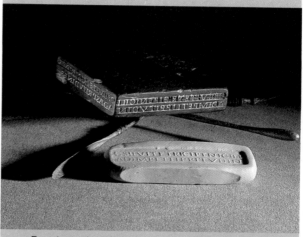

Eye doctor's palette, used for mixing ointments. His remedies are inscribed around the edge.

Tweezers for plucking eyebrows, nail cleaners, an ear scoop and a toothpick. The bone comb has fine teeth to trap nits.

1 Visitors undressed and met friends in the changing rooms.
2 After exercising, they went to the tepidarium (warm room) to sit or bathe.
3 The caldarium was hot and steamy. Bathers sat and used strigils to scrape off sweat. They finished with a hot bath.
4 Finally, they had a refreshing dip in the frigidarium (cold bath). Then oils and perfumes were rubbed into their skin.

In the shops

In the centre of every Roman town in Britain was the forum – the main business and shopping centre. Shops and offices formed three sides of a rectangle. On the fourth side was the basilica or town hall. The central space was filled with stalls on market day.

As towns grew, more shops were needed away from the centre. These were built along the town's main road or high street. The shops were small, with counters opening out on to the streets. They had wooden shutters that folded back instead of doors.

Weighing the goods

Official inspectors checked the goods that the shops sold and made sure that the measures were correct. The steelyard weighed goods by balancing the hanging pan with a weight that slid along the bar. The weight of the goods could be worked out from the markings along the bar. The Romans used the pound weight, *libra* (written today as *lb*), divided into 12 ounces (*unciae*). You might have used a balance for weighing at school. The Romans used similar balances – 2000 years ago!

Many shops were workshops too. The craftsman worked there and his family lived in small rooms at the back of the shop. This shoemaker made and sold leather shoes.

The banker counted his money using an abacus, a simple form of calculator. There was no paper money and a bag of coins was heavy. There were no newspapers either and so the pictures on coins were a way of spreading news throughout the Empire.

The seller of glass had beakers, bowls and bottles that came from Germany, Italy and even Syria. The glass must have been carefully packed for such a long journey.

Many families ground corn into flour and made their own bread. In the large towns, it was often easier to buy the flour, or even to buy the bread already baked. In London, large bakers' ovens and a large stone for milling corn into flour have been found. The millstone was turned by a donkey.

A steelyard for weighing goods. The object to be weighed would have been placed in a pan below the lead weight. Also missing is the weight that slid along the bar. The bar is marked at pound intervals and at 5 (V), 10 (X) and 20 (XX) pounds.

Roman coins of gold, silver and bronze. One coin informs the Empire of the continuing conquest of Britain.

Writing

There was no writing in Britain before the Romans came. The language the Romans spoke and wrote was called Latin. Most Romans learnt to read and write and soon some of the Britons learnt Latin too. Roman writing has survived in such things as books, business documents and letters. It can also be seen in inscriptions on statues and tombstones and in names scratched on pots.

Books were written by hand on scrolls. These were rolls of papyrus, a form of paper made from reeds. The books contained stories, histories and poems, but very few have survived and none have been found at Roman sites in Britain.

Writing a letter

Letters and business documents were written on very thin pieces of wood, using bronze pens and ink made from soot. Wooden writing tablets covered with a layer of beeswax were also used. A special pen called a stylus was used to form the letters on the hard wax, and mistakes could be smoothed out with the flat end of the stylus.

Letters scratched in wax on a fragment of writing tablet. They read *'Londinio'* – 'to London'.

Thin wooden panel with ink writing.

20

Two, three or more tablets could be hinged together with string. A string was wrapped round the whole bundle and held in place with a piece of wax called the seal. The owner used his finger-ring to mark the seal with a pattern. Anyone trying to read the contents had to break the seal.

Pieces of wood survive in wet ground if the air cannot reach them. Because of this, many pieces of writing tablets have survived in Britain. Often the stylus scratched through the wax on to the wood beneath. Sometimes it is possible to read what was written.

A pen and inkpot for writing in ink and a stylus, tablet and seal box. Wax seals were sometimes kept in boxes like this to protect them.

How many hands in a foot?

Roman measurements were based on parts of the body – fingers, hands, feet and paces.

Measurement chart
4 digits (fingers) = 1 palm (handspan)
4 palms = 1 foot
5 feet = 1 pace
1000 paces = 1 mile (*milia passuum*)

Write like a Roman

Using a sharp point, copy some of the letters at the bottom of the page on to a flat piece of Plasticine. How easy is it to write curved letters? Try writing a message.

Which letters of the alphabet were not used by the Romans?

Building a house

Although there were many towns in Roman Britain, most people still lived in the countryside. Wherever they lived, they used materials that could be found locally for building. Special materials, such as marble, were only brought in for important public buildings and splendid houses.

Fine houses had walls built of lumps of stone mixed with mortar, a kind of cement. Stonemasons cut the stone to shape. All the craftsmen had their own special tools. Many were similar to those used today.

Most houses had windows, small panes of blue-green glass set in wooden frames, while some had iron grilles as a protection.

The team of wall-plasterer and painter had to work fast. The plaster was smoothed on to the wall and the painter painted his design while the plaster was still wet. When it dried, the wall-painting had a hard shiny finish. When the walls needed redecorating, the old paint was covered with a thin layer of plaster, ready for a new design.

Mosaic floors were made using cubes cut from pottery, different-coloured stones and, sometimes, blue glass. These were put together to make up a beautiful pattern, sometimes showing pictures of people or animals. The man laying the floor sketched out the pattern in the wet concrete before he began work. Such floors took a long time to complete and were expensive. Only the rich could afford them.

Under the floors of the bigger houses lay the central heating system (*hypocaust*). Hot air flowed under the floors and up the walls in channels built of hollow tiles.

The public buildings and finer houses had tiled roofs, often made from local clay. There were also government tile works controlled by a Roman official called the procurator. The tiles were stamped with the letters PPBR, Procurator of the Province of Britain.

These tools belonged to a carpenter. The wooden handles have been replaced - the real ones had rotted away.

Archaeologists excavating a mosaic, at Milk Street, in London.

Wattle and daub

Poorer or less important houses were built with wooden frames. Carpenters cut timbers to make the frames. The gaps between the wooden uprights were either filled with mud bricks or smaller wooden twigs (wattle), and clay (daub) was applied to hold it together. The walls were then sometimes covered with plaster.

Roofs were thatched. With thatched roofs and timber frames, there was a great danger of houses catching fire, and many were destroyed in this way.

In the countryside

A villa estate

Most people in Roman Britain lived in the countryside. Some landowners lived in luxurious buildings at the centre of large farms, known as villa estates. The farmhouses often had colourful mosaic floors and wall paintings, underfloor heating (*hypocausts*) and bath houses. Other people lived on farmsteads that had few Roman features, looking like the houses the Britons had lived in before the Roman invasion. Slaves and farm labourers often lived in buildings away from the main house.

A room at Chedworth villa today. Can you see the piles of bricks that allowed hot air to flow under the floor, warming the room above?

Work on the farms

The people on the farm produced food and clothing materials for themselves and also to sell to people in the towns and abroad. Wheat and barley were grown in fields that had been ploughed by teams of oxen, and the harvested grain was stored in granaries. The tools used by farm workers were similar to those used by gardeners and farmers today. Only the metal parts have survived to be found by archaeologists – the wooden handles have rotted away.

Cattle, sheep and pigs grazed in the fields. In bad weather they were kept in shelters and barns close to the main house. To get extra food, people hunted and fished. The wool from sheep was spun and woven by women to make clothing.

A mosaic from a villa at East Coker, showing the return of the hunters with the deer.

Farm tools: (going clockwise) hoes, ploughshare, teeth from a rake, sickle, mattock and axe.

A British farmstead

Crafts and industries

When the Romans came to Britain, they brought with them objects and methods of making them that were new to the Britons. Soon the Britons learnt new skills from the Roman settlers.

Romano-British potters copied Roman pottery shapes and started using a wheel, which helped them create a better-shaped pot. The pots were decorated, sometimes with moulded patterns, sometimes with clay of a different colour. This was applied rather like piping the icing on a cake.

Some time after AD 70, glass vessels began to be made in Britain. When heated in a furnace, hot glass is very like runny treacle. This molten glass can be blown, like a balloon, into different shapes to make bottles, cups and bowls.

Blacksmiths worked lumps of iron in their forge, keeping the metal white-hot in their furnaces. They hammered the hot metal into different shapes, making axes, hammers, nails and chains.

Animal bones were carved to make combs, handles, hairpins, furniture hinges and needles. The craftsmen used tools such as saws, drills, chisels and lathes to make these objects.

Making a bronze statuette

1 A wax model is prepared.
2 The model is covered with clay. One area is left uncovered, as an opening.
3 The clay is heated. The wax melts and runs out through the opening.
4 Molten metal is poured in through the opening.
5 When the metal has cooled, the clay is broken open to reveal the statuette.

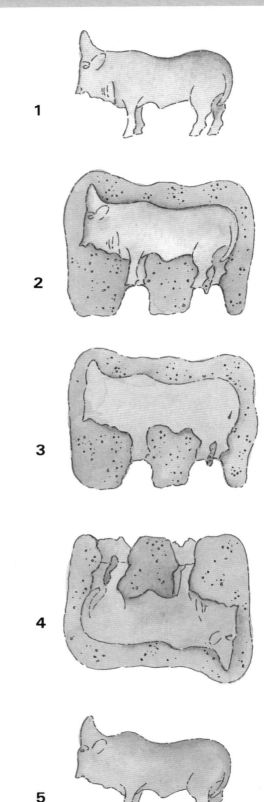

1

2

3

4

5

Down the mines

In England, the Romans found lead, tin and silver, and in Wales, they found some gold. Rocks that contain these metals are found below the ground. Roman engineers were skilled at designing mines. They used slaves to dig the shafts and tunnels and to hammer out the rocks. Slaves carried the broken rocks to the surface in baskets.

The rocks were crushed and heated to free the metals, and then the lumps of metal were heated until they became liquid. They were poured into shaped moulds and left to harden. These blocks of metal, ingots, were then sent to the metalworkers.

This lead ingot is stamped with the name of the Emperor Vespasian.

An altar showing Vulcan, the god of blacksmiths, with a pair of tongs.

Bone hairpins and a bone knife handle with an iron blade.

Eyebrows and ears have been stuck on this pot to make a face.

The stag on this pot has been put on like the icing on a cake.

Travelling around

The Romans are famous for the roads they built. Along these, the armies marched and relays of riders quickly carried official messages across the Empire. This meant the Emperor could easily stay in touch with his soldiers and governors.

Travelling on land

To go short distances, many people simply walked. For those who could afford it, travelling by horseback was the quickest way to get around. The wealthy had slaves to carry them on litters (beds or seats fastened between two long poles) and they also used covered wagons to travel longer distances. To carry their goods, farmers and merchants used two- or four-wheeled carts, pulled by mules or oxen. Transport by road was slow and wagons could not carry big, heavy loads. It was much cheaper to send large amounts or heavy goods by boat.

Soldiers building a road

The soldiers used layers of stones, pebbles, gravel and sand to make a firm foundation. The top layer of stones was curved slightly, so that rainwater would run off the surface.

Ships and boats

Boats relied on the wind to fill their sails and move them along, although warships were rowed by teams of slaves. Some boats had a rounded keel (bottom). The rounded keel made it easier for them to sail through the waves. Others had flat bottoms. These boats were used for sailing up and down rivers and through calm waters around the coasts.

Ships and wagons were made mainly of wood, rope and canvas – materials that easily rot away. Remarkably, the remains of two Roman boats – a flat-bottomed barge and a sea-going ship – were found preserved in the wet mud of the River Thames. We can discover more about how the Romans travelled by looking at pottery, wall-paintings and even mosaic floors, which were decorated with horses, ships and carts.

A skeleton of a Roman horse. Some of the bones on its spine are partly joined together. This might have been because it was ridden or pulled heavy loads before it was fully grown.

In this picture of a Roman waterfront, how many types of transport can you see?

This is a Roman barge, found near Blackfriars Bridge in London.

29

Buying and selling

Roman merchants created a wide network of routes to move their goods from one end of the Empire to the other. Goods were transported along the roads built by the army, along the rivers that linked the provinces and by sea.

The goods that the merchants brought to Britain were important in the early years after Claudius' invasion. Romans came to Britain to settle. They expected to be able to buy the same goods in Britain that they could buy in the rest of the Empire, but British craftsmen could not easily make what the new settlers wanted. Merchants quickly realised that they could make money by supplying the goods that people wanted.

In London, part of the town was a major port, built on the edge of the River Thames. From the quayside and warehouses of London goods were supplied to the rest of the province. Tableware and food were the main imports (goods brought in).

Goods from Britain

Before the Romans conquered Britain, it was rumoured that the province was rich in gold and silver. Only small amounts of these precious metals were found, but there were larger quantities of lead and tin. Lead was exported (sold abroad) as metal blocks, ingots. Wool was a much more important export. Production centres were set up to supply the Empire with woven woollen cloth. Slaves, hunting dogs and oysters were also sold to other parts of the Empire.

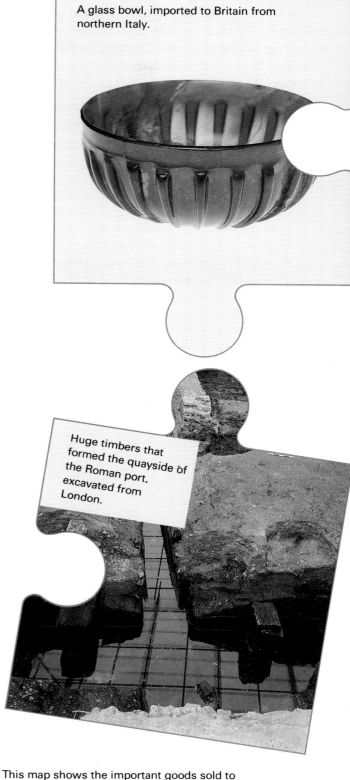

A glass bowl, imported to Britain from northern Italy.

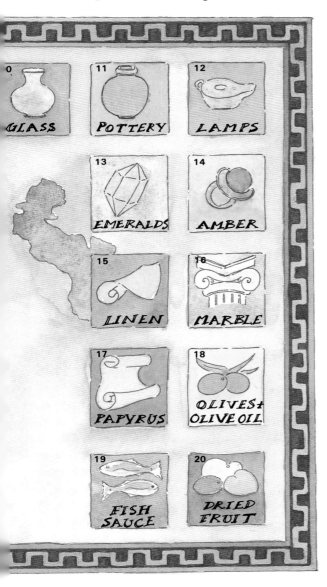

Huge timbers that formed the quayside of the Roman port, excavated from London.

This map shows the important goods sold to Britain from other parts of the Empire, and goods that Britain sold to other countries.

Citizens and slaves

Archaeologists have found evidence that shows where people lived and the sort of work they did. There is not much to show us what daily life was like for different groups of people. What we do know comes from written evidence from Roman Britain and other parts of the Empire.

The Romans divided people into different groups. There were citizens, who were full members of society and could vote in elections. At first, only Romans could be citizens, but as the Empire spread, the Emperor granted citizenship to non-Romans. There were also non-citizens and slaves.

Latin writing carved in tombstones and other stones gives us some clues about the people who lived in Roman Britain.

1 This tombstone tells us that Julius Vitalis was a soldier from abroad. He made armour and served in the Twentieth Legion.

2 Can you see the letters ANN.XV on this tombstone? They stand for the Latin for '15 years'. Marcus Aurelius Eucarpus was only 15 years and 6 months old when he died.

3 This writing gives us a clue about the work people did. It says, 'Good luck to the spirit of this place. Young slave, use to your good fortune this goldsmith's shop.'

Citizens in Britain

In the early days, many of the Roman citizens in Britain arrived to work in the government, in the army, or as merchants. Tombstones give their names and the country where they were born.

At first, Britons would not have been citizens, although they took Roman names and followed the Roman way of life. These people were the craftsmen, the shopkeepers, the labourers and those freed from slavery.

Slaves

Slaves were bought to work as servants in the houses, or in the businesses and on farms. They came from beyond the British frontiers. Some were treated badly and lived very hard lives. Others were valued for their skills and became craftsmen or clerks. They could save up to buy their own freedom or be granted freedom by their masters.

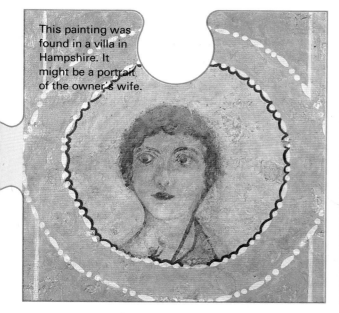

This painting was found in a villa in Hampshire. It might be a portrait of the owner's wife.

Family life

In the family, the father was the master of the household and everyone had to obey him. The family included the slaves and any other relatives who lived in the house. Women stayed at home as mothers and ran the household. If their parents could afford it, boys and girls went to school at the age of six or seven. They learnt to read and write, and also studied history and sports.

Sometimes, Roman life was not very different from our own. A letter has been found, sent from Claudia Severa, living near Hadrian's Wall. It invites her sister, Sulpicia Lepidina, to a birthday party on 10 September.

What's in a name?

A Roman citizens had three names: a first name, or Christian name; a family surname and a third name which was sometimes a nickname.
Marcus Aurelius Eucarpus
People who were not citizens had two names.
Sabidius Maximus
Slaves had only one.
Felix

Where is Julia from?

A This writing is from the tombstone of Julia Fortunata. It tells us she was a loyal wife to her husband, Verecundius Diogenes. Can you work out where she came from? (Answer on page 48.)

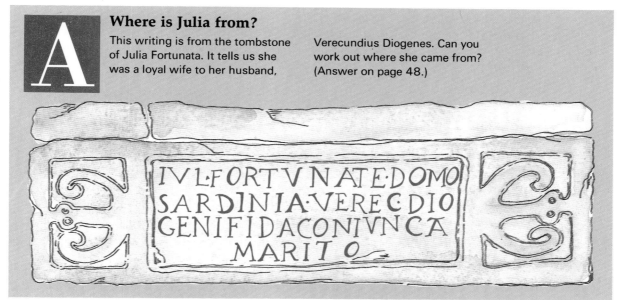

IVL·FORTVNATE·DOMO
SARDINIA·VEREC·DIO
GENIFIDACONIVNCA
MARIT·O

33

Togas and tunics

Pictures on tombstones, mosaics and wall-paintings give us an idea of what sort of clothes the Romans wore. Very few items of clothing have survived, except for those made of leather, such as shoes.

Most clothes were made from the wool produced by the British farmers. The woollen cloth was dyed red, blue, green, yellow and purple. The finest woollen cloth was worn by the rich, the coarsest by the poor. Finer materials, such as linen and silk, were brought in from abroad and so were expensive. Children dressed like their parents.

Men's clothes

Roman men wore a toga, a long semi-circular piece of cloth that wrapped around the body. It was worn over a knee-length tunic that had a belt. In Britain, togas were worn by a few wealthy men, on special, formal occasions. Normally, men wore tunics and warm woollen cloaks with hoods.

A letter written to a soldier has been found by archaeologists. He was based at Vindolanda, a fort on Hadrian's Wall. The writer of the letter was sending him socks, underpants and sandals, obviously to help him keep warm.

All the objects shown here might have been found on a lady's dressing table. You can see a lamp, two circular mirrors and a palette for mixing make-up.

Women's clothes

The women of Roman Britain wore long tunics fastened at the waist by a belt. Over the top they wore shawls. Both men and women used silver or bronze brooches to fasten tunics and cloaks. The brooches were often decorated with brightly coloured enamel.

Ladies' hairstyles changed according to the latest fashions, but were always based on long hair. The fashion was often set by the style worn by empresses, shown on coins. Hairpins kept the hair in place.

Shoes

Shoes were made of leather. Some were sandals made of one piece of leather that wrapped around the foot. Others were made with separate soles stitched to the upper parts of the shoes. Iron hobnails, nailed to the bottom of the shoe, protected the sole and made the shoe stronger in bad weather.

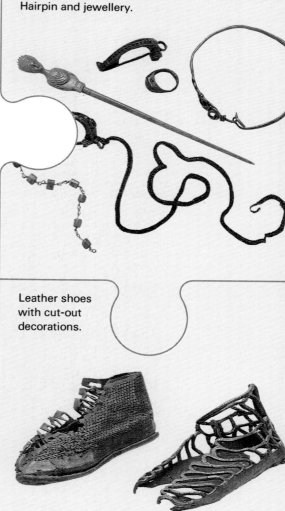

Hairpin and jewellery.

Leather shoes with cut-out decorations.

What's cooking?

The Romans enjoyed their food and, for the rich in Roman Britain, there was a wide variety, brought from all areas of the Empire. Many cookery books were written and one food lover, Apicius, recorded recipes of stuffed dormice, peacock rissoles and snails. Such recipes were only for special occasions.

The main meal was in the evening. Those eating the meal lay on settees around a low table in the dining room (*triclinium*). They were served by slaves and used their fingers to eat, instead of forks. Most people went to bed when it got dark. Their lamps used olive oil and the light they gave was poor.

This is a reconstruction of a Roman dining room. It has been built in the Museum of London.

Samian plates and bowls with knives and spoons. Food was eaten with the fingers.

Plates and bowls made of red glossy pottery came from France. All the richer houses throughout the Roman Empire had this popular tableware, called samian. It was expensive, so if it got broken, it was sometimes repaired rather than thrown away.

Eating cheaply

Poorer people in Britain had less choice of food and could not have afforded meat every day. They ate apples, pears, cherries and plums. Oysters were plentiful and cheap. The very poor ate a form of porridge.

In the kitchen

Plain jugs and bowls were used in the kitchen (*culina*). Pots and saucepans stood on iron grilles over slow-burning charcoal or were placed amongst the embers – like a modern barbecue. Other food dishes and bread were cooked in ovens heated by charcoal.

In this reconstruction of a Roman kitchen, you can see large storage jars (amphorae). These contained different foods. Some came from southern France and contained fish sauce, a kind of liquid salt made from fish and water. It formed the basic ingredient of most savoury recipes. Others contained olive oil used both in cooking and as lamp fuel. The oil came from Spain.

Pots from the kitchen: the large bowl (*mortarium*) with its inside roughened with grit was used for grinding up ingredients.

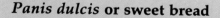

Panis dulcis or sweet bread

A You might like to try this Roman recipe. Ask an adult to help you to heat the oil.

For one:
1 thick slice of white bread
65 ml milk
oil for frying
1 tbsp clear honey

Remove crusts and cut bread into cubes. Place in basin and pour milk over. Leave for ten minutes. Heat oil in frying pan. Add bread cubes and fry until golden. Drain on kitchen paper. Pile in a dish and pour honey over.

Entertainment

The Romans brought new types of public entertainment to Britain. Open-air theatres, semi-circular in shape, were built in the newly founded towns. Funny plays (comedies), sad plays (tragedies) and mimes were performed in them. Actors wore masks as part of their costume.

Amphitheatres were oval-shaped arenas, also open-air. They were large enough to seat the whole town. The amphitheatre was used for religious ceremonies, gladiator fights, animal baiting and acrobatic displays. It could also be used by soldiers as an exercise ground.

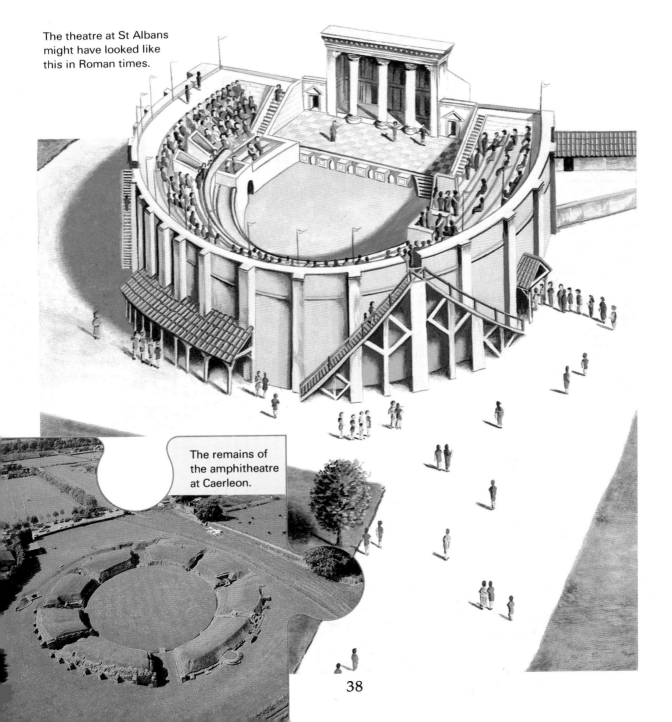

The theatre at St Albans might have looked like this in Roman times.

The remains of the amphitheatre at Caerleon.

Gladiators

Male slaves were sometimes bought especially to be trained as gladiators (professional fighters). In gladiator schools, they learnt how to use different kinds of weapon for fighting. Gladiators were given special names, depending on which kind of weapon they used. The *retiarius* specialised in fighting with only a net and a trident, while the *secutor* wore a helmet and used a sword.

Gladiator fights were exciting but bloody, because the loser was usually killed. If he had fought very well, the loser was sometimes given a 'thumbs-up' sign by the watching crowds and the officials. This meant his life was to be spared. Thumbs-down meant death. Successful gladiators were often able to save enough money from their winnings to buy their freedom and retire.

Toys and games

At home, people amused themselves in many ways. Children played with dolls, wooden hoops, balls, spinning tops, miniature weapons, board games and pets. They were taught to play musical instruments such as lyres and pipes. Grown-ups used dice for gambling games. They also enjoyed hunting deer and wild boar.

Some toys and games were made of wood and cloth that rotted away when placed in the earth. Objects were not needed to play some games, such as leap-frog or hide-and-seek; there is no evidence for archaeologists to find. So how do we know what games were played? Luckily, the Romans wrote about many of them, and some are shown on surviving mosaics, wall-paintings and decorated pottery.

This pottery vase was found at Colchester. It shows gladiators fighting. Their names are Memnon and Valentinus.

A toy dog, found at Kirkby Thore, in Cumbria.

Bone dice and shaker.

The gods

The Romans believed in more than one god. Each of their gods and goddesses controlled a different area of daily life. The Romans also adopted local gods worshipped in other parts of the Empire and sometimes even made their emperors, living and dead, into gods.

Every day, the Romans said prayers at their household shrines to Vesta, goddess of the home, and to the Lares and Penates, the guardians of the family. They also prayed in temples, where statues of the gods and goddesses were kept. Animals were killed as sacrifices on stone altars.

Each god had a holy day or festival when celebrations and public games were held. A priest or priestess in charge of the temple received offerings and sacrificed animals. People gave what they could afford.

A popular festival was the Saturnalia, held in mid-December in honour of Saturn, god of farming. People gave each other simple gifts, houses were decorated and slaves swapped roles with their masters for a day.

Christianity

Some religious groups were banned by the Roman emperors. Christianity was at first regarded as a dangerous secret society and Christians in Rome were put to death. Christianity did not become the official religion of the Empire until AD 312.

Archaeologists have found very little evidence for Christianity in Roman Britain. At Lullingstone villa, pieces of wall-plaster show Christians at prayer and a Christian church has been found at Colchester. A floor mosaic has been found at Hinton St Mary in Dorset. It shows the face of a person, and some people think it is meant to be the head of Christ.

I am Neptune, god of the sea. Sailors pray to me.

I am the sun god Mithras, from Iran. Roman soldiers and merchants worship me.

I am Jupiter, king of all the g[ods]

I am Diana, goddess of the moon and hunting. I deliver babies safely.

My armour shows that I am Mars, god of war.

People seeking love, pray to me. I am Venus, goddess of love and beauty.

I am Juno, Jupiter's wife.
I am goddess of women.

I am Minerva, goddess of wisdom.

I am Mercury, the winged messenger of the gods.

Which planets of the solar system are named after Roman gods?

The temple of Mithras

The god Mithras was first worshipped in Iran. The Roman soldiers and merchants who worshipped him spread the cult throughout the Empire. Only men were allowed to take part in the ceremonies. In London in 1954, an archaeologist discovered the remains of a temple of Mithras. As well as the remains of the temple, some fine marble sculptures were found. They were sculptures of Mithras and of other gods worshipped in the same temple.

This head of Mithras was found in his London temple.

41

Death and burial

The Romans believed that people went to another world when they died – the Underworld, which was ruled over by the god Pluto. To reach the Underworld, the dead had to cross the River Styx. Dishes of food and flagons of drink were buried with the bodies, to provide food for the journey. Money was buried too, to pay the ferryman, Charon, to boat them across the river.

Cemeteries

The Romans had strict rules about where to bury the dead. The cemeteries were placed outside the town limits, usually beyond the town walls and alongside the main roads that led out of the town. This was a custom which they continued in Roman Britain. It was there that all the dead from the town were buried, rich and poor. The rich built stone buildings called mausolea to house their dead. The poor had simpler burials. Often, tombstones were erected to mark the spot.

Looking at tombstones

 Roman tombstones gave similar information to tombstones today.

This is the tombstone of a Roman soldier, found near Corbridge in Northumberland. He is a medical orderly (*medicus ordinarius*) in a cohort of the Roman army. Can you fit the English translation on the right to the Latin on the left? Compare the Roman tombstone with the modern one in the middle. How does the information differ?

IN MEMORY OF
JOE BLOGGS
SOLDIER OF THE
5th HUSSARS
DIED 1. 1. 1916
AGED 25
R.I.P.

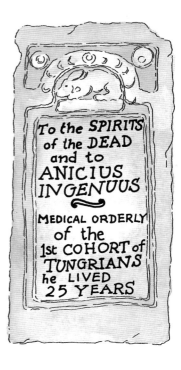

To the SPIRITS of the DEAD and to ANICIUS INGENUUS MEDICAL ORDERLY of the 1st COHORT of TUNGRIANS he LIVED 25 YEARS

Cremation

For the first 200 years that the Romans were in Britain, it was the fashion to cremate the dead. The ashes were placed in a pot. Some cremations were placed in specially purchased glass urns, others were put in old cooking pots or even large round storage jars. The pots were then buried in the ground, with the food placed beside them.

A cremation pot with lamp within a tile box from Colchester.

Examining skeletons

Cremation went out of fashion and the people of Britain were either buried in a rectangular pit, or in coffins made of wood, lead or stone. They were buried with their clothes, jewellery and treasured possessions, as well as food.

Their skeletons have often survived to be excavated by archaeologists. By examining the bones and teeth, it is possible to say whether it is the skeleton of a man or a woman and to say how old the person was when they died. The objects buried with the body can also help archaeologists to decide whether it was a man or a woman, and perhaps whether they were rich or poor.

Looking for clues

A Look at these pictures of bones found in a Roman cemetery in Britain. What do you think the objects are next to the skull? Do you think this is the skull of a man or a woman? Can you see any objects in the other picture? (Answers on page 48.)

The Romans leave Britain

The Romans ruled Britain for nearly 400 years but it was not always easy. The province of Britain was surrounded by lands that were not part of the Roman Empire and Britain was often attacked. There were arguments as to who should rule the Empire and local army leaders declared themselves emperor and seized power.

One of these leaders was Carausius, the admiral of the British fleet which protected the English Channel from pirates. He declared himself Emperor of Britain and Northern France in AD 286. Seven years later, he was murdered by his financial adviser, Allectus. Allectus then declared himself emperor. By now the real emperors, based in Rome, were tired of these pretenders and soldiers were sent to get rid of Allectus. The Roman army won the battle and returned Britain to the Roman Empire.

Raiders from Scotland and Ireland attacked from northern and western Britain.

A line of forts were built around the south-eastern coast of Britain to keep the raiders out.

1 BRANCASTER BRANODUNUM
2 BURGH CASTLE GARIANNONUM
3 WALTON CASTLE
4 BRADWELL OTHONA
5 RECULVER REGULBIUM
6 RICHBOROUGH RUTUPIAE
7 DOVER DUBRIS
8 LYMPNE LEMANIS
9 PEVENSEY ANDERITA
10 PORTCHESTER PORTUS ADURNI

Coins of Carausius and Allectus. Each declared himself to be Emperor of Britain.

NORTH SEA

JUTES

Saxon pirates from across the North Sea attacked southern Britain.

ANGLES

SAXONS

FRISIANS

FRANKS

Protecting the Empire

The Romans had to build extra defences in Britain to keep out raiders from Ireland, Scotland and northern Europe. They built forts along the coast and strengthened towns, but as other parts of the Empire came under attack from barbarians (foreigners), some of the legions left Britain to fight elsewhere. They never returned. The province was left with fewer soldiers to protect it, at a time when more and more raiders were attacking the country.

There was no great ceremonial departure. By AD 410, Rome itself was being attacked and the Emperor Honorius simply refused to send any more soldiers to defend Britain. They were needed elsewhere in the troubled Empire.

Life went on as usual for some time. Gradually, towns became deserted and fell into ruins. Life continued in the country, where the Saxons settled in alongside the Britons.

The Roman fort at Portchester in Hampshire, built to repel the Saxons.

Roman Britain and life today

The Romans left their mark in many different ways on all the countries that had been a part of their Empire. The most obvious evidence of a country's Roman past are the buildings, which in some countries are still in use. Roman beliefs and customs still play a part in our lives today.

This arch is in Lincoln. In Roman times it was one of the town ga

When was it built . . . ?

In Britain, the most famous visible remains are the walls that the Romans built to defend the province. Hadrian's Wall is the most important. Many town walls are Roman too, but later repairs often hide the Roman work. Other Roman buildings lie hidden under our present streets. It was often easier to build over them than to demolish all the ruins.

What does it mean . . . ?

Latin, the language of the Romans, still survives in written form throughout Europe. Doctors and lawyers, for example, use Latin words and phrases in their work. Many words and names in the English language come from Latin words. Roman numbers are still used too, especially for dates. The year is often shown in Roman numbers at the end of a film or television programme.

What's the date . . . ?

The calendar we use today was organised by Julius Caesar in 45 BC. He changed the start of the year from March to January and declared that there would be 365 days in a year, with February having an extra day every fourth year. The names of the months are based on the original Latin names.

Januarius – from Janus, the two-headed god of doors, looking at the old and the new year.
Februarius – from a Roman festival.
Martius – from Mars, god of war
Aprilis – from Latin, 'to open', spring
Maius – from goddess Maia
Junius – from goddess Juno
Julius – from Julius Caesar
Augustus – from the Emperor Augustus
September – from Latin for seven, originally the seventh month
October – from Latin for eight
November – from Latin for nine
December – from Latin for ten

Roman numerals

1 = I	6 = VI (5 + 1)	20 = XX
2 = II	7 = VII	50 = L
3 = III	8 = VIII	100 = C
4 = IV (5 − 1)	9 = IX (10 − 1)	500 = D
5 = V	10 = X	1000 = M

The date 1992 written in Roman numerals is **MCMXCII**. How would you write the year 2020 in Roman numerals?

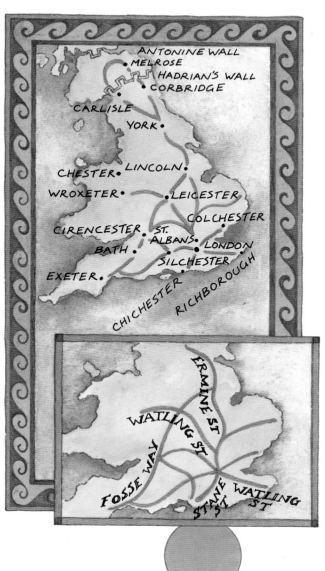

Where did they come from . . . ?

The Romans introduced new plants to Britain, including peas, carrots, cucumbers, cabbages, walnuts, cherries, mulberries and figs. Archaeologists have excavated their seeds. Traces of a wide range of vegetables and other plants have not survived, because the plants were eaten before the seeds could form. We know about them from reading Roman recipes.

Which way to . . . ?

The Romans gave their towns in Britain Latin names and these form the base for their modern names. Many modern roads follow the routes along which the Romans built their roads. The A1(M), for example, which runs from London to York, was originally the Roman road we call Ermine Street. The Romans put up milestones that signposted the distance between the towns. The custom of using signposts still exists.

You can see the line of the old Roman road, the Fosse Way, in this photograph.

Index

*Numbers in **bold** indicate illustrations.*

Answers

Page 33: Julia is from Sardinia.
Page 43: Picture A shows a woman's skull. The objects are hairpins. Picture B shows a ring on finger bones.
Page 46: 2020 is MMXX in numerals.

Published by BBC Educational Publishing, Woodlands, 80 Wood Lane, London W12 0TT

First published 1992
Reprinted 1993, 1994

Paperback ISBN: 0 563 34999 9
Hardback ISBN: 0 563 35000 8
Typeset by Ace Filmsetting Ltd, Frome, Somerset
Colour reproduction by Daylight Colour, Singapore
Cover origination in England by Dot Gradations

Printed in Great Britain by

BPC Paulton Books Limited

Photo credits

Ancient Art and Architecture Collection **pages 16 (right)**; British Museum, **page 5**; Cadw: Welsh Historic Monuments, Crown Copyright **page 38**; University of Cambridge, Committee for Aerial Photography **pages 14, 47**; Colchester Archaeological Trust **pages 10 (right), 43 (bottom)**; Colchester Museums **pages 7 (bottom), 9 (top), 10 (left), 39 (top), 43 (top)**; Dorset Natural History and Archaeological Society, Dorset County Museum, Dorchester, Dorset **page 9 (middle)**; English Heritage **pages 8 (bottom), 15, 45**; Lincolnshire County Council: City and County Museum **pages 46/47**; Museum of London **pages 7 (top), 11, 13 (bottom), 16 (left), 17, 19, 21, 23, 25 (bottom), 27 (middle and bottom), 29, 31, 35, 36, 37, 39 (bottom), 41, 44**; The National Trust **pages 13 (top), 24**; Somerset County Museums Service **page 25 (top)**; Tullie House Museum, Carlisle **page 39 (middle)**; Winchester Museum/Hyde Historic Resources Centre **page 33**; The Yorkshire Museum/Jim Kershaw **page 27 (top)**.

Front cover: Michael Holford

Illustrations © Ray Grinaway 1992 pp 4-5, 8-9, 16-17, 28, 38; Lorraine Harrison 1992 pp 2-3, 11, 20-1, 26-7, 30-1, 32-3, 42, 44-5, 47; Sally Hynard 1992 43, 40-1; Peter Kesteven 1992 6-7, 12-13, 14-15, 18-19, 22-3, 24-5